A Practical Guide for Your Kid's Mental Health

Staying Awesome and in Control

Ronald Diaz

Copyright

Table of content

Introduction

Chapter 1: Fundamentals of Children's Mental Health

Chapter 2: Nurturing Positivity and Confidence

Chapter 3: Cognize Changed Behavior in Your Child

Chapter 4: About Birth Defects

Chapter 5: About Behavior Disorders

Chapter 6: Mental Health Games for Children

Chapter 7: Make Sure You Take Care of Yourself As Well

Conclusion

Introduction

It is frequently simpler to understand the physical demands of a kid when it comes to the effort to properly supply nutritional food, drink, warmth, and so on. When it comes to the mental health of a kid, the parent may not have such an easy time at all. A kid's mental health may not be as visible as his or her physical condition or wants, therefore their parent would have to be aware of the issue of mental health development before even attempting to comprehend the child's progress. Get all the facts you need here.

Chapter 1:

Fundamentals of Children's Mental Health

Preview

An excellent good mental health situation would be where the child can think clearly in various gatherings and learn new skills to acclimatize to the surrounding needs of the time and also be confident with improving his or her confidence level, high self-esteem and an emotionally stable perspective on life.

The Fundamentals

In the attempt to comprehend as well as provide well for the child's healthy mental growth the parent should be able to provide factors such as love and acceptance from the relatives, teach the child confidence level and high self-esteem standards, and spend as much hours as possible with the child to motivate social interaction and growth so that the child will be comfortable in knowing how to extend the same to other new additions whenever and wherever introduced.

By spending the time to connect more with the kid via play and other forms of contact, the parent will also be able to help the child to learn how to take advice and encouragement from other sources such as instructors and supportive caregivers.

It will also allow the youngster to recognize a safe and secure setting in which to engage with others. With the necessary direction and discipline, the kid will be able to make all the diverse choices required for good mental health development.

Chapter 2:

Nurturing Positivity and Confidence

Preview

Self-esteem is frequently associated with the mental process; this is a vital factor in encouraging the optimum development of a child's positive and confident attitude and perspective. This will also be the contributing component to the cerebral development and corresponding social adaptation of the youngster.

Self-Confidence

One of the key contributions a parent can make to establishing this in a kid's growing process would be to guarantee there are also good parenting methods employing love, care, and respect as the cornerstone of building a confident and social youngster.

When a youngster is taught to look at themselves and learn to accept and enjoy what they see looking back at them, then the route to acquiring confidence will be set.

Making the kid realize how vital it is to be able to accept oneself and only select good improvements to make should there be a need for adjustments should be part of the nurturing process given by the parent.

It is crucial to constantly take the time and effort to reaffirm the need to establish a strong self-confidence attitude in the youngster, and this can be done with a lot of good remarks and encouragement.

From even as early as the infancy stage, the little one will be able to perceive its self-assurance when the appropriate responses are given to its various cries.

Children too will gradually catch on to this as they learn how to perform things according to what is appropriate and so experience the consequent good nurture and praise that will assist to also increase their confidence levels.

In getting this attention anytime the infant screams out for it, the initial steps to gaining confidence will be made. Although at this moment, the newborn truly does not grasp the relevance of its cerebral progress.

Children too will gradually catch on to this as they learn how to perform things according to what is appropriate and so experience the consequent good nurture and praise that will assist to also increase their confidence levels.

Chapter 3:
Cognize Changed Behavior in Your Child

Preview

Every parent should be mindful of any modifications in behavior patterns a kid may demonstrate as they might give substantial information to the parent on what is truly going on in the child's head and therefore his or her environment.

What Is Different

There are various advantages to being able to spot these changes and this capacity to read into the changes might sometimes be the only method a parent has available to aid in how manage a certain circumstance.

Most medical specialists would confirm the fact that a kid's primary exhibit of a given behavior is generally developed by tying numerous lesser actions together.

Helping the kid deal with or enjoy a certain scenario would help a very lot if the parent was able to accurately recognize the behavioral pattern, therefore allowing the parent to offer the necessary proportional aid to the child.

In attempting to comprehend the child, the parent would have to eagerly observe the different reactions and displays of emotions as this will nearly always clearly indicate the child's train of thought or needs thus trying to contribute to an inevitably more unified collection of behavioral habits that can be more readable.

The kid will also learn to utilize the parent as their major example by monitoring the parents' diverse emotions and behavioral patterns and in certain circumstances opting to emulate these with as many parallels as possible.

Therefore the parent would have to be extremely cautious in how they express their behavioral patterns as they should be continuously conscious of the children's capacities and comprehension levels of replicating such displays.

Through such observations, the parent will be able to better deal with the numerous varieties such as a strong will kid, a child who has to be competitive constantly, and a child that requires a lot of encouragement and supplies the necessary lessons as required.

Chapter 4:
About Birth Defects

Preview

All parents are interested in the many elements of the children and this generally starts right from the moment of conception, and usually never stops. Perhaps one of the first worries would be about any potential birth problems the kid may be born with and how to deal with as effectively as possible should this be the case.

What Can Happen

Birth defects are commonly defined as any predominant anomalies of anatomy, function, or body metabolism that may or may not be visible at the time of birth.

For the more visible anomalies, the appropriate supporting teams will be able to aid the parent in either learning how to manage the birth defect or help the parent explore all alternatives available if any, to repair the issue as soon as it is permitted.

The structural or metabolic flaws would be focused mostly on certain body components that are either missing or malformed in some manner which may be caused by some issue with the body chemistry that was unable for some reason to develop a full and flawless kid in the womb.

These deformities commonly include instances of spina bifida, cleft palate, clubfoot, congenital dislocated hip, and many more possibilities.

The problems induced by congenital infections may frequently result in abnormalities when the mother encounters an infection before or during the pregnancy stage.

These diseases will cause birth malformations and might be in the form of rubella, CMV, syphilis, toxoplasmosis, Venezuelan equine encephalic, parvovirus, and chicken pox.

The pregnancy phase is normally a time when care should be made to reduce the risks of the mother having to struggle with the assault of deceases that may have highly detrimental consequences on the baby.

Unfortunately, this presence of deformity is not always attributable to any virus as even apparently healthy parents are occasionally delivered with a kid with visible abnormalities.

Chapter 5:

About Behavior Disorders

Preview

All kids at one point or another have some type of behavioral difficulties, it is normally fairly an accepted standard that most parents are usually able to live with. However, when a certain behavior pattern becomes constant and damaging, aid should be sought in recognizing and repairing the issue so that all parties will be able to cope.

Behavior

The more frequent and not actually hazardous or highly detrimental behavioral problems would include extremely active youngsters getting into trouble, pulling pranks, being sometimes rebellious, and other milder behavior patterns.

However when these lesser patterns take on a more severe and ominous show of negativity then they can no longer be regarded as normal but instead should be looked at as behavior disorders.

The much more widely accepted initial symptoms of such negative and often inappropriate behavior would be hurting or making threats to themselves, pets, or others, managing or vandalizing property, lying or pilfering, not doing well schoolwork, and even avoiding school, early smoking, and alcohol and drug use, young sexual activity, regular tantrums and arguments and consistent antipathy towards people in positions of authority.

All the aforementioned shows would surely imply a problem kid and the parent would nearly always be at a loss on how to manage in such instances.
The uncertainty and anger felt by both parties should be handled adequately so that progress can be made to try to overcome this negativity and assist the kid to embrace the idea of help to return to a calmer and better behavior that others can live with.

A recent study has been able to reveal that it is not always outer conditions that contribute to the bad behavior patterns but may occasionally be related to some disease in the brain.

Lack of specific chemicals or simply the imbalances of chemicals in the brain might be one of the explanations for the behavior being experienced therefore the need to study this option also.

Chapter 6:

Mental Health Games for Children

Preview

Working with children who have mental health difficulties may be fairly tough and adding to this would be the complexity that most of these youngsters would not be eager and receptive to the aid being offered owing to their mental illness. Therefore utilizing games as a stimulating aspect would be a fantastic and motivating tool to start with.

Some Tips

These games may readily be discovered and bought online or at any gaming retailer. Due to the diversity accessible, the parent would have to evaluate the kid's mental state and what it would require to excite it in the greatest manner feasible.

It is not always required to acquire these games since some may be created or developed only from some intuitive creativity to meet the demands at hand.

Board and card games are a typically wonderful methods to engage the intellect. These boards' activities are generally particularly created to treat the mental health difficulties the kid may be experiencing such as depression, self-esteem issues, attention deficit hyperactivity disorder, and many more.

These board games may also be employed from a therapeutic viewpoint which would encourage the youngster to be part without being compelled to tackle

the real mental health problem straight on. It may also contribute to helping the kid practice some of the social skills that most mental health problems youngsters shy away from.
This will also ultimately assist to address the self-esteem difficulties the youngster may be going through. The parent may also employ typical games but with the extra function of asking the youngster to make one positive comment about themselves each round they play.

Strategy games may also be especially valuable tools as they also serve to increase the self-confidence of the youngster throughout the process of improving problem-solving ability and improving functioning as a team.

Chapter 7:

Make Sure You Take Care of Yourself As Well

Preview

Exercise in the form of walking, jogging, cycling or swimming is encouraged. If you are over the age of fifty, running is not encouraged as it will place a pressure on your joints particularly on the knees. Swimming is the finest type of exercise for all age groups and you may do this any time of the day. Just half an hour of swimming is plenty.

It Takes You Too

Our body demands a certain amount of relaxation a day. When you have a kid with you, you will notice that you are quickly weary owing to the anxiety of making sure the child is fed, the child is secure and the child is receiving enough rest.

You will be awake at all hours to care for the youngster. All these activities will put a toll on you and make you feel exhausted. Try to get adequate rest whenever possible. Even half an hour of sleep will do you good.

Another key to keeping a healthy mind and physically is a good diet.
You must ensure that you acquire all the nourishment in the form of vitamins, fibers, carbs, and protein in balanced meals and supplements.

These meals and vitamins will guarantee that your body gets what it needs and this will in turn maintain the mind healthy and bright.

Conclusion

To provide your kid with the finest health and mental care possible, you have to be physically and psychologically well to do so. When you are not one hundred percent, your mental and physical state of mind will not be able to monitor and identify any deviation in your child's physical and mental sociability. That is why you must have a regular schedule of exercise, relaxation, and diet to keep a decent physical and mental condition.

Note.

www.ingramcontent.com/pod-product-compliance
Lightning Source LLC
LaVergne TN
LVHW020544160826
845677LV00015B/4200

9798848655070